Introducing Psychology

How to Improve Life through Applied Psychology Principles

Change Your Mindset, Create Success, Initiate Positive Change, End Procrastination

By Noah Grayton

Introducing Psychology

Published by:

CyberLearners, LLC.
14837 Detroit Avenue #202
Cleveland, OH 44107

Legal Disclaimer:

Furthermore, the transmission, duplication or reproduction of any of the following work including specific information will be considered an illegal act irrespective of if it is done electronically or in print. This extends to creating a secondary or tertiary copy of the work or a recorded copy and is only allowed with express written consent from the Publisher. All additional rights reserved.

The information in the following pages is broadly considered to be a truthful and accurate account of facts, and as such any inattention, use or misuse of the information in question by the reader will render any resulting actions solely under their purview. There are no scenarios in which the publisher or the original author of this work can be in any fashion deemed liable for any hardship or damages that may befall them after undertaking information described herein.

Additionally, the information in the following pages is intended only for informational purposes and should thus be thought of as universal. As befitting its nature, it is presented without assurance regarding its prolonged validity or interim quality. Trademarks that are mentioned are done without written consent and can in no way be considered an endorsement from the trademark holder. This book is not giving medical advice.

Table of Contents

Introduction

Because we are frequently exposed to the work of psychologists in our everyday lives, we all have an idea about what psychology is and what psychologists do. In many ways your conceptions are correct. Psychologists do work in forensic fields, and they do provide counseling and therapy for people in distress. But there are hundreds of thousands of psychologists in the world, and many of them do other types of work

Many psychologists work in research laboratories, hospitals, and other field settings where they study the behavior of humans and animals.

Psychologists also work in schools and businesses, and they use a variety of methods, including observation, questionnaires, interviews, and laboratory studies, to help them understand behavior. This chapter provides an introduction to the broad field of psychology and the many approaches that psychologists take to understanding human behavior. We will consider how psychologists conduct scientific research. We will look at some of the most important approaches used and topics studied by psychologists. You will learn that psychology is a field that will provide you with new ways of thinking about your own thoughts, feelings, and actions.

Despite the differences in their interests, areas of study, and approaches, all psychologists have one thing in common: They rely on the scientific method. Research psychologists use scientific methods to create new knowledge about the causes of behavior. Practitioners, such as clinical, counseling, industrial-organizational, and school psychologists, primarily use existing research to help solve problems. In a sense all humans are scientists. We all have an interest in asking and answering questions about our world. We want to know why things happen, when and if they are likely to happen again, and how to reproduce or change them. Such knowledge enables us to predict our own behavior and that of others.

We may even collect data, or any information collected through formal observation or measurement, to aid us in this undertaking. It has been argued that people are "everyday scientists" who conduct research projects to answer questions about behavior (Nisbett & Ross, 1980). When we perform poorly on an important test, we try to understand what caused our failure to remember or understand the material and what might help us do better the next time. When our good friends Monisha and Charlie break up, we try to determine what happened.

When we think about the rise of terrorism around the world, we try to investigate the causes of this problem by looking at the terrorists themselves, the situation, and others' responses.

The Problem of Intuition

The results of these "everyday" research projects can teach us many principles of human behavior. We learn through experience that if we give someone bad news, he or she may blame us even though the news was not our fault. We learn that people may become depressed after they fail at an important task. We see that aggressive behavior occurs frequently in our society, and we develop theories to explain why this is so. These insights are part of everyday social life. In fact, much research in psychology involves the scientific study of everyday behavior (Heider, 1958; Kelley, 1967). Unfortunately, the way people collect and interpret data in their everyday lives is not always scientific. Often, when one explanation for an event seems "right," we adopt that explanation as the truth. However, this reasoning is more intuitive than scientific. Intuition is thinking that is more experiential, emotional, automatic, and unconscious, and does not lead to careful analysis of all the variables in a situation (Kahneman, 2011).

Other explanations might be possible and even more accurate. For example, eyewitnesses to violent crimes are often extremely confident in their identifications of criminals.

People may also believe in extrasensory perception (ESP), or the predictions of astrology, when there is no evidence for either (Gilovich, 1993). Furthermore, psychologists have also found that there are a variety of biases that can influence our perceptions. These biases lead us to draw faulty conclusions. In addition, most individuals listen to people they know and trust to give them accurate information rather than doing research to determine what scientific studies show.

In summary, accepting explanations for events without testing them thoroughly may lead us to think that we know the causes of things when we really do not.

Hindsight Bias: Once we learn about the outcome of a given event, such as when we read about the results of a research project, we frequently believe that we would have been able to predict the outcome ahead of time. For instance, if half of a class of students is told that research concerning attraction between people has demonstrated that "opposites attract" and the other half is told that research has demonstrated that "birds of a feather flock together," most of the students will report believing that the outcome that they just read about is true, and that they would have predicted the outcome before they had read about it. Of course, both of these contradictory outcomes cannot be true. In fact, psychological research finds that "birds of a feather flock together" is generally the case. The problem is that just reading a description of research findings leads us to think of the many cases we know that support the findings, and thus makes them seem believable.

The tendency to think that we could have predicted

something that has already occurred that we probably would not have been able to predict is called the hindsight bias.

Why Psychologists Rely on Empirical Methods

All scientists, whether they are physicists, chemists, biologists, or psychologists, use empirical research to study the topics that interest them. We can label the scientific method as the set of assumptions, rules, and procedures that scientists use to conduct empirical research. Empirical research methods include collecting, analyzing, and interpreting data, reaching conclusions, and sharing information

Chapter 1: Psychology Defined

Psychology is the study and science of the mind and behavior. It is an umbrella term that includes many multifaceted subjects. It is an academic discipline with a huge scope of practice and study.

The study of psychology developed out of a need to study the mind. It may seem at first glance that we didn't get around to studying our minds as a human race until the 1800s. However, this is not the case. In fact, the philosophers and ancient theologians of history were addressing psychology in their own way. The human species has had its methods of addressing psychological problems since the dawn of time, but it took us a lot longer to start a formalized study of the mind.

Psychology is rooted in many different disciplines, including philosophy, science and art. The philosophy connections come from the impulse to think about problems and examine our thinking processes. Psychology has a great weight on moral issues of our time. Whenever a practice is as rooted in moral implications as psychology, there must be philosophical considerations. When we do philosophical studying, it prepares us to think. It doesn't teach you what to think, but rather how to think. Being able to think and work out problems coherently is important for not only Psychology but other fields as well.

Psychology is closely aligned with science because one of the goals of the study of psychology is to measure and explore and investigate the mind, behavior, and emotion. This exploration can often best be done by employing the scientific method. The scientific method provided a huge foundation for the advancement of psychology, and without science, there would not be the field of psychology, as we know it today.

It is, of course, a meta-oriented study; how can you study something when you must view it through the subjective lens of what you are studying? Psychology, in its most basic form, tries to develop an objective view and measurement of the mind's processes, patterns, and development. The only way we can engage with the subject, however, is by using our human, subjective minds, which, as we know by now, are very limited to our personal experience and perspective. So, we are put in a bit of a bind. Our task is to be objective and scientific in the study of the mind, but we are forced to use our minds to do the studying, and we can't trust our minds to be objective. It is this catch-22 with which we proceed as we venture into the study of psychology.

The study of psychology can basically be broken down into two methods: the quantitative and the qualitative.

Quantitative study is the method that wants to have clear measurements of everything and only look at things that are measurable. For example, a cup of water measured in a measuring cup- this is a quantitative measurement. We can see how much water is in the cup, we can measure it with pre-existing tools, and we know from our experience of using the tools that they are pretty accurate. Therefore, we can be pretty confident in the fact that the cup of water is a cup of water. Quantitative measurements can be applied to psychology. This mostly comes from behaviorism, and this sect of psychology is centered on using measurements of mental and emotional phenomena. One way this might be done is by using a depression questionnaire, or answering ratings about different aspects of your experience, i.e., on a scale of one to ten, how anxious are you?

Qualitative study in psychology is rooted in phenomenology. Phenomenology is the perspective of studying experience. Rather than trying to get quantifiable data out of a situation, the phenomenologist will ask for descriptions of what the experience was like for a person. Qualitative study looks at our subjective experience and embraces the subjective, rather than trying to draw out data to provide empirical results. Qualitative study often takes the form of essays, interviews, case studies, and other forms of research. An opinion piece is usually mostly qualitative.

Psychology is the study of the mind, but what does the mind entail? The mind is a concept that is still argued to this day. What are the limits of the mind? Is there a difference between the mind and the brain? What domains are controlled by the mind? Is there a soul? These are questions that are still debated, and which still affect the study of psychology. The mind is the genesis for our thoughts. It is also the "control room" for the body. The mind encompasses the brain, which is the physical "hardware" that carries out tasks for the mind. The mind is like computer software, but a thousand times more intelligent than we could imagine and a thousand times more creative than we could imagine a computer to be. The mind is a somewhat nebulous concept. It comprises our thoughts and directs our emotions. Our thoughts and emotions are functions of the mind. Emotions have a strong physical component but are still processed through and directed by the mind. The human mind is the most wondrous concept that we can possibly think of. It is the highest level of evolution. It is the apex of intelligence, creativity, love, and thought. The study of psychology, then, is very important.

Psychology is an attempt to diagnose what is "normal" and what is "pathology." Pathology occurs when someone has developed in a way that is not functional or has symptoms that cause problems in their lives. Pathology is essentially" sickness of the mind. Pathology could be presented as negative thoughts, hallucination, or any other symptoms. When psychology also helps us to know, when pathology is found, how to treat it. If someone's pathology is that they are depressed, psychology says that we can put them through treatments to help get better. There are a variety of therapies and medications that exist for the treatment of mental and emotional health problems.

Of course, we are now developing knowledge on why it's important not to overdiagnose and not try to pathologize behavior that does not do harm. If you think about the history of society's' beliefs and development, you can see how attitudes have changed over the centuries. It was once believed immoral for women to wear anything but dresses. Once, we didn't understand electricity. So, we are a part of our cultural and time context, and that will affect our psychology. What was considered pathological behavior fifty or a hundred years ago is now known to be natural. The attitudes of what is expected of people in western culture are fairly restrictive, even in our day and age. Psychologists in our contemporary age should take caution not to just slap a diagnosis on every difficult or weird behavior. The diagnosis is really not that important to understand people. Understanding people comes from using your intuition and being a compassionate person. The diagnosis is just some words that needed to be labeled for reference for healthcare providers and the general public. There is no need to classify someone as certain type of person because of his or her diagnoses.

Indeed, there may be many more people around you with a diagnosis of a mental health disorder or illness than you think. There are certain conditions, like schizophrenia, depression, anxiety, or other disorders that can be very hard to detect in casual conversation with someone. Schizophrenia is one that we think of as being a very serious disease; with the symptoms of a crazy person with hallucinations and talking voices. This is not the truth. There are certainly extreme cases of schizophrenia that cause people to have very bizarre behavior, but there are many, many people living with mild or moderate cases of schizoaffective or schizophrenia disorder who are very functional and live in work in the same space as we do.

Psychology is an essential and important study. We need to be able to look at the mind from an outside perspective and try to find out what is going on. This is not only for the treatment of pathology but also for the advancement of our human species and the well-being of our communities.

Psychology's Central Questions

Psychology has changed dramatically over its history, but the most important questions that psychologists address have remained constant:

- **Nature versus nurture**: Are genes or environment most influential in determining the behavior of individuals and in accounting for differences among people? Most scientists now agree that both genes and environment play crucial roles in most human behaviors. Yet we still have much to learn about how nature, our biological makeup, and nurture, the environment and experiences that we have during our lives, work together. The proportion of differences that is due to genetics is known as the heritability of the characteristic. We will see, for example, that the heritability of intelligence is very high (about .85 out of 1.0), but we will also see that nature and nurture interact in complex ways. Given this complex interaction, psychologists now consider the question of how they interact to produce behavior as more relevant than whether nature or nurture is more important. •

- **Free will versus determinism**: This question concerns the extent to which people have control over their own actions. Are we the products of our environment, guided by forces out of our control, or are we able to choose the behaviors we engage in? Most of us like to believe that we are able to do what we want. Our legal system is based on the concept of free will. We punish criminals because we believe that they have choice over their behaviors and freely choose to disobey the law. But as we will discuss later in the research focus in this section, recent research has suggested that we may have less control over our own behavior than we think we do.

- **Conscious versus unconscious processing**: To what extent are we conscious of our own actions and the causes of them? Many of the major theories of psychology, ranging from the Freudian psychodynamic theories to cognitive psychology, argue that much of our behavior is determined by variables of which we are not aware.

- **Differences versus similarities**: To what extent are we all similar, and to what extent are we different? For instance, are there basic psychological and personality differences between men and women, or are men and women by-and-large similar? What about people from different ethnicities and cultures? Are people around the world generally the same, or are they influenced by their backgrounds and environments in different ways? Personality, social, and cross-cultural psychologists attempt to answer these classic questions.

- **Accuracy versus inaccuracy**: To what extent are humans good information processors? It appears that people are "good enough" to make sense of the world around them and to make decent decisions. But human judgment is sometimes compromised by inaccuracies in our thinking styles and by our motivations and emotions. For instance, our judgment may be affected by emotional responses to events in our environment.

Chapter 2: History of Psychology

Early Psychology

The earliest psychologists that we know about are the Greek philosophers Plato (428–347 BC) and Aristotle (384–322 BC). These philosophers asked many of the same questions that today's psychologists ask. They questioned the distinction between nature and nurture and the existence of free will. Plato argued on the nature side, believing that certain kinds of knowledge are innate or inborn, whereas Aristotle was more on the nurture side, believing that each child is born as an "empty slate" in Latin a tabula rasa, and that knowledge is primarily acquired through learning and experience.

European philosophers continued to ask these fundamental questions during the Renaissance Period. For instance, the French philosopher René Descartes (1596–1650) also argued in favor of free will. He believed that the mind controls the body through the pineal gland in the brain, an idea that made some sense at the time but was later proved incorrect. Descartes also believed in the existence of inborn natural abilities. A scientist as well as a philosopher, Descartes dissected animals and was among the first to understand that the nerves controlled the muscles.

He also addressed the relationship between mind, the

mental aspects of life, and body, and the physical aspects of life. Descartes believed in the principle of dualism; that is, the mind is fundamentally different from the mechanical body. Other European philosophers, including Thomas Hobbes (1588–1679), John Locke (1632–1704), and Jean-Jacques Rousseau (1712– 1778), also weighed in on these issues. The fundamental problem that these philosophers faced was that they had few methods for settling their claims. Most philosophers did not conduct any research on these questions, in part.

Edward Titchener helped create the structuralist school of psychology. Their goal was to classify the elements of sensation through introspection.

But dramatic changes came during the 1800s with the help of the first two research psychologists: The German psychologist Wilhelm Wundt (1832–1920), who developed a psychology laboratory in Leipzig, Germany in 1879, and the American psychologist, William James (1842–1910), who founded a psychology laboratory at Harvard University.

Many ancient civilizations researched the topics of philosophy, but it was not named as such. Ancient philosophy tends to deal with matters of the mind, and Socrates' method of questioning to find the truth rings true today. The questioning method is one of the foundations of talk therapy. There were philosophers in ancient Africa which discussed emotions, the habits of the mind, depression and thought disorders.

There are many parallels with the traditions of ancient Greek philosophers, ancient African philosophy, and ancient Buddhist philosophy. Buddhism is based on the teachings of the Buddha, which emphasize the middle path and detachment from self. These teachings, when viewed through the lens of the history of psychology, were an early example of man's tendency to look in on himself. By creating a detachment to the self, the Buddhists were embracing a way of thinking which let them stand back and observe the mind. The practice of mindfulness, which stems from ancient Buddhist practices, is popular today as a method of self-regulation and bolstering mental health. There exists a text from ancient Buddhism entitled "The Yellow Emperor's Classic of Internal Medicine," which discusses theories of personality based on the yin and yang balances, mental disorders and wisdom.

The Enlightenment in Europe around the 16th century was a time when psychology, helped along by Gottfried Leibniz, advanced as an area of study. Christian Wolff published important books on the topic, and Immanuel Kant mentioned the subject as well.

You've probably heard of studies involving rats, designed to modify their behavior. These types of studies have been tried over an over again with different hypotheses and subjects. These methods of studies are labeled as experimental psychology. This all began in Germany in the 1830s, when Gustav Fechner started taking measurements of human stimuli perception. Once these initial studies were begun, of what we are experiencing and recording when perceiving data, the practice of experimental psychology exploded and psychologists all over the world started practicing with experiments that were designed in similar or different ways which started the establishment of experimental psychology.

Back in the 1800s, there was a psychology society called La Societe de Psycholgie Physologique in France. This consisted of scientists, psychologists, and other thinkers, who would meet to share thoughts and research about psychology. The American Psychological Association was founded just before the dawn of the 20th century.

Wilhelm Wundt used scientific research methods to look at human reaction times to stimuli. He published a book called "Principles of Physiological Psychology," which talked about the connections between the science of physiology and the study of thought at behavior. Wundt thought that the study of psychology was the study of consciousness. He thought that you could use science experiments to study the internal processes.

Edward Titchener was a major figure in American psychology. He was a student of Wundt's and came up with the theory of structuralism. He thought that you could break down human consciousness into smaller patterns. He used the process of introspection to train people to break down their responses and thoughts into measurable metrics.

American psychology at this point was still somewhat crude; the study of eugenics was still a standard topic in psychology classes. During WWI and WWII, the U.S. military established itself as a leading funder of psychology research and application. Psychology became a way for the government to influence the people. Psychologists had a big role in the management of the economy, as well.

Around the early part of the 20th century, Sigmund Freud was developing his method of psychoanalysis. This totally changed the landscape of the treatment of mental disorders. Freud was largely responsible for the formalization of talk therapy. This also established the case study technique.

The most major development in psychology after psychoanalysis came in the '40s and '50s with the study of behaviorism. Behaviorism can be known as a system of psychology but also as a sort of philosophy. This was a big shift from the previous theories that were prominent in psychology. Before behaviorism, most psychologists studied the conscious and unconscious mind. Behaviorism changed thing up, and behaviorists strove to make psychology a more scientific practice. They wanted only to look at observable behavior. Observable behavior could be a dog ringing a bell or a mouse hitting a button when he knows he will get a reward.

Rounding out the 20th century, around the '60s and '70s, came Third Force Psychology. This was centered on the thought of Carl Rogers. Car Rogers is known as one of the founders of this school of thought. Rogers took some cues from psychoanalysis but focused more on the power of free will and self-determination. Maslow is also a big name in Third Force psychology; he created a hierarchy of needs that described the needs of people throughout development. The Third Force psychologists focused more on phenomenological study. They were more interested in discussing the experience and understanding the subjectivity of the mind. They also believed in the concept of self-realization, the thought that in each of us, there is a" true" or "authentic" self, which can develop through personal development practices.

Psychology today has many strains of thought and philosophy. There is a big emphasis on CBT, cognitive behavioral therapy, which incorporates aspects of behaviorism but tempers it with cognitive theory. There is DBT, developed in the '70s for the treatment of borderline personality disorder by Marcia Linehan. DBT is one of the more modern treatment approaches. It emphasizes coping, mindfulness, and skills are learning.

This is where we are with psychology today: we have a couple of centuries of history. It's not much; especially if you consider how long some other formal studies have been around, like mathematics and art. However, we've come a long way in the past couple hundred years, and there is still more to go. The psychology field today is rich and diverse, with lots of different options and strains of thought. Some of them go together nicely, and some of them disagree. Psychology now has become a reflexive study, one that considers a sense of self-awareness about its past and context

Psychology and those who study it should be considerate of the cultural context of its ideas and patients. People don't exist in a vacuum. People are very complicated, and they are deeply affected by the environments they grew up in. People who grow up in rural areas might have different traditions that those who grew up in urban areas. People of different races have different cultural values and different traditions. Throughout psychology, women have not been sufficiently represented, in research or prominent roles. Psychology research has been unfairly centered toward males. These are all considerations that have to be taken into account when forming a new theory on psychology. For someone with a particular cultural value, they might think of body language in the form of contact, like hugging, to be invasive. Another person, however, could've grown up with a family that considered hugging normal. They both are fine, and either way is a find way to grow up, and one shouldn't be preference over the other. This is just one example of a small cultural difference that could lead to a divide.

These kids of multicultural considerations and postmodern topics are at the forefront of psychology right now. Psychologists are now realizing the depth and meaning of family of origin and cultural context, and are starting to learn how to employ methods to be inclusive to all sorts of people from different ethnicities, religions and backgrounds.

Chapter 3: Famous Psychologists and Their Movements

Out of all of the characters that exist in the history of psychology, Sigmund Freud might be the most influential of them all. His "talking cure," talk therapy, revolutionized the treatment of mental disorder and started the field on a path of treatment that is still essential to this day. Freud developed his theory of psychoanalysis after years of working in medical settings. He was influenced by many factors, including mysticism and philosophy.

Sigmund Freud was born in Moravia, in the Austrian Empire. This is the area that would later be labeled as the Czech Republic. His father was a wool merchant, and Sigmund had two brothers. The family was Jewish, and the children were raised in that tradition. Eventually, the Freud family found themselves struggling, and they left Freiberg, where they had been living, to move to Manchester, England.

Sigmund Freud went to the University of Vienna when he was seventeen. He joined the medical department, and worked with brains and zoological subjects, and helped to discover the neuron in the brain. When he became an MD, he started working at Vienna General Hospital. He did research on the brain and was a published and accomplished writer. He kept working in various areas of medicine, spending time in psychiatric clinics and asylum. He was appointed the prestigious position of lecturer at the University of Vienna.

Freud eventually resigned at the hospital and started a private practice. He described his work as specializing in nervous disorders. One of Freud's colleagues, Brentano, had introduced him to the concept of the unconscious mind. Along with this, he had done other research into the philosophy of the unconscious. There are many analogies between Freud's work and Nietzsche, but Freud claims to not have had Nietzsche as an influence.

His most important work, arguably, is the development of psychoanalysis. Freud went to Paris to study with a renewed neurologist. This visit was a catalyst for him to turn toward the practice of psychology and away from his neurological research. Freud started experimenting with hypnosis. The results of his hypnosis work were inconsistent. He started coming up with ways to get patients to free-associate. Free association is when you say whatever comes to mind, with no filter. Freud thought that instead of making suggestions to people through hypnosis, he could let them talk freely and he could analyze the structure of their unconscious material. He thought that repression was the root of pathology. Psychoanalysis was the term that he started to use to describe his new method. In psychoanalysis, Freud believed that he could retrieve subconscious information that can help people understand their thought process, in order to change it.

Alfred Adler was a psychologist who was working around the same time as Freud, but just a little later. He is classified as a psychotherapist. Psychotherapy is "talk therapy." It is often known as counseling. Adler took many ideas from Freud and was inspired by his work. Adler met with Freud in 1907 and became the president of the Vienna Psychoanalytic Society. Freud thought of Adler as a student and disciple of Freud's, but Adler didn't see it that way. He made his ideas separate from Freud's. Adler had a different way of interacting with patients; whereas Freud would have the patient lie down and free-associate. Adler started to become more relationship-centric, he was a pioneer in the field of talk therapy.

Jean Piaget was a psychologist from Switzerland, who did a lot of groundbreaking work in the area of childhood development. Piaget was educated in the psychoanalytic stain of psychology. He went to a school that was led by Binet, who had created the IQ intelligence test. Piaget helped to design and administer the IQ test. He noticed, when giving the test to children they made certain types of mistakes that adults did not make. This served as part of the foundation for his work. Piaget is most known for his stages of childhood development. The theories mostly have to do with cognitive and sensory perception. Piaget's stages are very interesting to learn about and can clue you into meeting children where they are and understanding how they experience the world.

B.F. Skinner was a psychologist and one of the most important figures in the study of behaviorism. He was a professor a Harvard and developed some very important concepts to the field of psychology. One of these concepts is Operant Conditioning. This is a method of learning that is based on punishment and reward. There can be negative punishment and positive punishment; in this context, positive and negative have different meanings than usual. Negative in this context means taking something away. This could be a punishment or a reward. For example, positive punishment is adding something to the subject that is unpleasant, like spraying a cat with a spray bottle of water. Negative punishment would be taking away something that is pleasurable, for example, taking away a child's toy when they have been misbehaving. Skinner solidified the concepts of operant and classical conditioning. This had a huge impact on how psychologists were able to frame their research. This gave psychologists the philosophical support they needed to claim that their experiments were worth doing, and it helped them to prove that they were making progress. Behaviorist is all about measurability and objectiveness.

Similarly to Piaget, Erik Erikson is best known for his work in the research of development of humans. Erikson's theory, however, includes the entire lifespan, whereas Piaget's mostly looks at childhood development. Erikson's stages start at infancy and break down the lifespan from there.

The stages of Erikson are fascinating, and can also tell you a lot about where you are in your life. Until eighteen months, according to Erikson, we are in the Trust vs. Mistrust stage. This is where an infant learns to trust the world and their caregiver. This is an essential stage, where a person learns that the world is not only dangerous but also contains multitudes of love. From eighteen months to three years is the stage of Autonomy Vs. Shame and Doubt. In this stage, the infant must accept that they are not one with the mother anymore, and they have a separate body and consciousness that they are living in. Three to five years is the Initiative vs. Guilt stage. This is where the child is learning to interact and transport themselves, and at this stage, they must navigate the challenges of both initiative and guilt and incorporate an understanding and tolerance for each. The next stage is five to thirteen years old, and it's the struggle of Industry vs. Inferiority. At this stage, children are learning new things and to become good at them. They might be playing sports or participating in the competition of relationships that high school often is. They may have pressure from their parents to do well in school or to work. The next stage is Identity vs. Role Confusion. In this stage, young people start to develop their identity in the world, and they must integrate a sense of identity to avoid the feeling of confusion, which happens when a person is not fully integrated with the experiences they have had in the past and their current emotional and mental life.

The next stage is Intimacy Vs. Isolation. This stage is where a person has hopefully developed an identity which they can have with a sufficient amount of detachment. What comes after this is the ability to be deeply intimate with people. This could be a marriage, or it could be reflected in friendships or other relationships. The ages from forty to sixty-five reflect the struggle of Generativity vs. Stagnation. This is a stage where a person has developed an identity and a sense of self-security and starts to have the need to "generate" life or creative projects into the world. The great struggle in this phase is to feel like one's life is productive. After sixty-five, Erikson suggests that the final phase of life is Ego Integrity Vs. Despair. People at this age either will be able to cope with the realization that death is upcoming, or they will find themselves despairing.

Chapter 4: How the Mind Works

The human mind is unlike anything else. It is a control center receiving signals from nerves, body parts, muscles, tendons, organs, and automatically processing the appropriate responses, learning, and growing. The mind is an impossible place to understand. Many disagree about what the mind is.

The Materialists, for example, would argue that nothing exists outside of the brain. There is an atheist, science-centered viewpoint that postulates that there exists nothing outside of the physical, real material of the world, like our bodies and observable things like the sun, earth, other people, etc. They say that there is not consciousness floating somewhere in an aura-like haze around a person and that the experience of consciousness is a product of the brain. The mind for the Materialists is the human experience of the brain working and directing our bodies.

Others point to a soul and minds that is altogether a different metaphysical existence than the brain. The brain and body exist in a real material world, where the mind and soul exist in a real non-material one. This argument of duality manifests in all kinds of forms in the arguments about what we are and what our consciousness is.

One thing that we can establish for sure is that we exist. Don't get caught up in all that talk about a simulation. Sure, that is a useful analogy for consciousness, but to actually believe that we are a brain in a vat? Well, you would have to adjust to that reality. And it might actually not be so different than your goals and aspirations in life. Even if it's all a simulation, there isn't a way to break out of it that we know of. People have tried all kinds of drugs and explored the consciousness in many chemically-induced methods. Spiritual experiences are reported to be authentic ways that we can break out of this reality. But for most people, the spiritual philosophy is a case-by-case factor; so in effect, we will perpetually be living in this reality. There is no easy long-term escape.

There is one "healthy" alternative: mindfulness and meditation. Mindfulness occurs when you are paying attention to the body and only the experience you are having in the vert present moment. Practicing mindfulness can help people to escape the mind, to have an opportunity to look in rather than out, and to realize important thoughts about themselves.

The mind, first and foremost, is resultant to our experience. If we are fed with education and learning at a young age, this will influence how we develop. Context is everything. Cultural traditions, language, and all kinds of other difference shape the diversity in our minds. There is, however, a common thread: Human consciousness.

The mind is always changing. Any of the information that enters through the five senses may make its way to the unconscious or the conscious memory. Each little experience is encoded somewhere in the brain, or determined not important enough to keep. The human being is a sensory animal who has evolved to be able to detect others and itself, see, hear, and smell predators, to enjoy or not enjoys experiences, along with countless other functions.

Our sensory input is how we experience the world. If you are talking about the "brain in a vat," then the sensory input is all the information that a person would need. It is through this filter that we find our way in the world.

One side of the argument says that we should be wary of the info that we get through our senses. There are several perspectives on this. Firstly, when we dream, most of us are completely tricked into thinking that the dream is reality. It is only when we awake that we find our bodies are still lying in our beds and that none of this has happened. But when we are dreaming, that is our reality. There is no way to say that what you experience in a dream isn't real, it's real in the moment. It may not be real to anyone else in the universe at that particular second, but it is still real to you in that moment.

Now, some people have reportedly developed the skill of becoming aware when they re dreaming. This is an interesting skill that has been widely reported as possible. However, the main point remains: that the sensory input of dreams is very convincing, and it is one area that points to the fallibility of our senses. Most of the time, they are pretty trustworthy, or so it seems. When you see something that you are going to walk into, and you walk into it and feel the pain as it bumps against your head, you are experiencing the true-ness of your senses. You sensed in your vision something that blocked your path, and you have evidence, the pain, that your vision was reality.

Another perspective is about how illusory real stimuli can be. People can make paintings that, when viewed from a certain angle, create the illusion of a hole in the ground of a skew of perspective. Visual illusions are present everywhere from art to the atmosphere to visual lines in the distance.

Another factor is emotion. You never know when emotions are affecting a person's perception. The level of intensity of some emotions can be incredible, and it can cause a drastic change in perception for a person.

So we have to take a mediated stance on whether or not to trust the senses. We must acknowledge that they can be tricky and that the senses will often mislead us. How many times in the past has this happened to you?

The mind can also be a predictable thing; how many people do you know that do the same thing every day? We tend to have habits and lifestyles, and we generally stick to the way we like to behave within that lifestyle. Habits and lifestyle are intertwined, and making changes to one can lead to changes in the other.

The mind generally is driven towards a few things: love, work, financial, career and pleasure. First of all, love is a major drive because it is what totally sustains the human race. It is what sets us apart from all other animals, and it is the force that drives our creativity, our power, our imaginations and our stability. It is everything, and love is why we are humans. The relationships that we make reflect the need we have to love others and be loved. For many people, this will eventually take the form of a dyadic relationship with other persons, with a commitment to love. For some people, they may never find a long-term relationship, or might not want to. Others might have taken on polyamory. Whatever position you are in, people usually have the common thread of needing to form relationships and have love in their lives.

The second drive, work, is not synonymous with money. The drive towards work could be a creative pursuit or a job that doesn't necessarily pay well. The drive to work is an inherent one in humans. It needs to be refined and helped along, but ultimately humans are creative beings, and we are also equipped with bodies that are designed and evolved to do work. In ancient times, we had to do work just to find food and protect ourselves from predators, and now we work because we need to support our families and ourselves financially so we can live in society and function in society. Our bodies are designed to function this way, and we need to use our bodies for their functions to stay sane in this life.

The next category of basic human drives is art. Art may seem like the least important category, but it is not. Art is a nonverbal way to process the world, to communicate with other people, to be with other people, to spread messages, to arouse emotions, to tell stories, etc. Some people think that without art or music or literature life would be okay. They think that it would go on like normal, and things would just continue, and that we have a lot more time for work. This is not the case. If there were not art, music, literature or movies; there would be a complete collapse of society, we could not handle it. Music and art is the way that we are able to be humans in the world and cope with what life has dealt us. We use it to understand the world, to express ourselves, to get by. We also use it to educate. Art transformed the history of philosophy and philosophy and art are deeply intertwined. Philosophy is the mother of all study, and philosophy is deeply tied with the artistic sensibilities.

The ultimate nexus of work, love, and art is, of course, creating a child. It is the ultimate creative expression. This is a creation that has all the capacity in the world. All the potential energy and output into the word exists in this person. The power to create a person is a devastatingly important and consequential one. This is something that people may have a huge ant of anxiety over. And rightly so, as it is a decision with great moral weight. How can we even comprehend what this "new" human will do, what they will become, what they will think? What if they do horrible things in the world? What if they aren't happy? However, we are somewhat destined to want to create in this way. Reproduction is coded into our DNA, and we all know the powers of the sexual drive. There is some way that we are inherently, as humans, bound to eventually get to this level of creation, that of another human, as we take care of our needs and progress in life.

Chapter 5: Psychology to Improve Your Life

How can you use psychology to improve your life? Well, first you have to determine what you need or what you need to change. This can be a difficult process, and sometimes, this ends up being the important part anyway. What are the problems that you are having with yourself or others?

Sometimes learning about personality types can help clear things up. There are lots of different resources about personality types, and having a guide to read through can help you realize what kind of person you are and can also help you to read other people. The Enneagram is a system of personality which presents many points about personality.

The Anagram presents 9 different personality types.

The first is The Reformer. This person is someone who is a perfectionist and wants everything to b good and cool and perfect. This personality type usually is very charismatic and often ends up in leadership positions.

The second type is the Giver. The Giver loves being able to provide for people. They are selfless, sometimes a little too selfless, and they like to be in certain roles, namely the helping ones. The Giver will sometimes be hard to draw out of their shell; they might think more about others that like to talk about themselves.

The next is the Achiever. The Achiever loves pushing things to the limit and doing the best they can. They are also very charismatic and get the party started. The Achiever is a big doer and has a lot to say.

Next is the Romantic. The Romantic loves art and rainy days and poetry. They might be into weird movies or want to spend a lot of time doing creative pursuits. The Romantic's flaw is that they can be very self-centered and sometimes overwhelming to themselves and others.

The next personality is the Investigator. The Investigator loves to ask questions and get to the bottom of things. They like to perceive and are very oriented to the perceiving side of things. They like to size people up and try to figure them out. Usually, they are good at this.

Number seven on the Enneagram of personality is the Loyalist. The Loyalist is often very loyal and loves to maintain family and close friend relationships. They may be overdependent on people, and they may get into codependent relationships as well.

Number eight is the Challenger. The Challenger is a strong person who is often oriented to helping other people by being forceful or aggressive. Their intentions are to help, but sometimes they do not know their own strength. It's not meant just as physical strength; Often the Challenger s a person of great psychic or emotional strengths.

Last is the Peacemaker. The Peacemaker is an old soul and has some similar characteristics to the Romantic. They like to search for meaning in things and seek justice. They have a natural tendency toward harmony.

This is just one of many systems of personality. You can look through these lists of characteristics and see what matches up for you. You may find that you strongly identify with one of these types, or you might find that you match up with two or three. Sometimes, you might need someone else to point out similarities that they see in you that you don't see.

If you have problems in your life that you're struggling to address on your own, it's recommended that you find a therapist that works for you. Not every therapist will work for everyone, but it is possible to find a therapist that you like and trust. This is a really important phase of getting treatment. Some people think of therapy as only being or people who are really crazy and weird. This is just not true. There are people from all walks of life in therapy, and they all are at different levels. Yes, some people have schizophrenic symptoms such as hallucinations or paranoia, but there are tons and tons of people who don't have extreme symptoms, they are just looking to improve their life. If you or someone you know is resistant to going to therapy (when you have the time and resources), you should ask yourself some questions. First, ask yourself "What are the biases that I might hold in my mind for therapy and people who go to therapy? Why don't I think that I deserve help with problems I may have in my life? What is my idea of counseling, and why am I resistant?

When you meet a counselor or therapist for the first time, you should try to be natural and be yourself, for any resistance up will just prevent you from recognizing in the person is a good match. People have all kinds of different relationships with therapists. Some discuss issues that cut to their core. Some people just want advice, or to be listened to. Some people like to keep their relationship very professional. Others are very personal with their healthcare professionals and like to laugh and joke with them. At any rate, you should find what works for you. Whether it's a male or female, young persona or older person, there is a therapist out there that will be able to help you. Don't give up if the first experience you have with a mental health professional is bad! I promise, they're not all bad. Some people are forced to go to therapy when they are children, and they associate it with the unpleasant feeling of not being in control of your doings.

Go to a few sessions, and see what you think of the work you have done so far. At this point, the therapist should have helped you to identify what you are working on and how you are going to work on it. This should involve you making plans with the therapist rather than them making all your goals and aspirations up for you. The work has to be authentic, and has to be real, and has to come from you. It can't be that your wife wants you to go to therapy and you don't want to, but you decide to go anyway just t satiates her. It has to be coming from you if you want to change.

Lots of people have trouble with automatic negative thoughts. This is a clear-cut case of an epidemic in the U.S. Many people are raised not to believe in themselves, and for whatever reason, whether it be family of origin, media pressures, personal pathology that is unaddressed, or other sources of origin, they have a lot of automatic negative thoughts flying around in their mind. There are many ways to address this.

CBT is a great way to address automatic negative thoughts. Remember, CBT means cognitive behavioral therapy. There are three main points that CBT considers: thoughts, feelings, and behaviors. So, if you are having trouble with parts of your behavior, CBT can help you to look at your thoughts and feelings around those behaviors and change them to help change your behavior. Or, if you are feeling disordered in your feelings, you can use CBT to look at your thoughts and actions and try to change your experience of your feelings by looking at the other factors in the "triangle."

Chapter 6: Basic Human Behavior and Mindsets

Human behavior can be known as a set of responses and drives. We have basic drives as humans: to eat, to sleep, to reproduce, to protect ourselves, and to build community. These drives are reflected in our behavior in many complex ways. Our behavior is also shaped by the demands that are put upon us. There is a range to the acceptability of behaviors; some behaviors are common and accepted, and there is a lot of behavior that falls outside of these lines. These lines are constructed collectively by society, and they are developed to keep people "in line" and behaving a certain way. This is what we mean when we talk about social norms and expectations. In this chapter, we will talk about some basic patterns of human behavior and mindsets.

One of the basic patterns of behavior and mindsets is addiction. Addiction is a pattern of behavior, which has good and bad aspects. All behaviors have a list of pros and cons, as to why they are healthy behaviors and why they are unhealthy behaviors. Smoking cigarettes, for example, is a behavior that has pros and cons. It is a way to spend time, to potentially be mindful, to have conversations, to loosen up. It also causes physical harm to your lungs and other parts of the body. This is an addiction that many people are struggling with right now in the county and the world. Each individual has to weigh the benefits and negatives of participating in this addiction. Some people understand the physical harm and still decide to smoke. Others smoke because they do not understand the physical damage that is being done.

Addiction can come from many places but is a somewhat mysterious and befuddling scientific and medical topic. It has been called by some a "spiritual" ailment. Some people would argue that this conception of addiction is dangerously unscientific, and they might be able to offer up some very compelling arguments. However, I believe it is the case to at least concise that this might be possible. The definition of addiction as a "spiritual" ailment might be stage, but it captures some of the nebulous nature of the disease.

Addiction can look many different ways and have a multitude of presentations. They all have common threads, however. Think about this: which addictions can make you lose your job? Booze, drugs, sex? Probably. Food, maybe. In its extreme form, food addiction can interfere with people's ability to work. This is especially true with people with eating disorders.

Let's try another: Which addictions can make you run out of money? Booze and drugs? Yes, those can cost a significant amount of money. Sex addiction? Yes, that can cause you to lose money. Food addiction? Yes again. Let's try another: Which addictions can kill you? Booze and drugs are a yes. Overdose can be lethal. Sex addictions? There are multiple scenarios in which a sex addiction and the behaviors that it causes can cause someone to end up dead. It is just the facts. Food addictions can lead to diseases and ultimately death.

Do you see what I'm getting at here? There is a commonality in all addictions. We get the first hit; we want more. We get the second hit; we want even more. We go on like this over and over, and the behavior is repeated and rewarded and repeated and rewarded.

Let's talk about the basic human behaviors and mindsets associated with depression.

Depression is a collection of symptoms. These include lack of motivation, trouble sleeping, sleeping too much, eating too little or too much, isolation and other possible symptoms. Lack of motivation is big one. It gets people stuck in a cycle. They don't feel good about themselves and don't want to do anything, and then they don't do anything, and then they feel bad about themselves for not doing anything. The cycle goes over and over. It is difficult to treat because when you have the lack of motivation induced by depression, you don't necessarily know that you have it. It is just something that has taken over your consciousness. The lack of motivation to get better is a part of the problem. So how do you induce motivation in someone?

There exists a concept that states that action precedes motivation. This is an interesting concept because it takes what appears like it should be backward and puts it forward. Most people think that motivation precedes action; you think about why you want to do something, and then you go and do it. This concept says that action precedes motivation. This means that you must act when you are NOT motivated.

If you can get a person to understand this, it could have an effect on their course of that mindset. What you try to get them to understand is not that you need to be motivated, because then you will take action, but it is actually that you need to take action, because then you will be motivated. It is a small phrase, but it has huge implications. That phrase put-into-action can cut through the haze of apathy that is sometimes created by depression, and in cases of severe depression, that haze of apathy can be all encompassing and crippling.

A mindset is a hard-to-describe thing. Mindsets could be confident; they could be lazy. Your mental makeup is always changing and adapting to every moment, and yet has very automatic features. This is part of the condition of duality that we are all in. We have to learn to balance one part with another part. For example, you have the motivation to do well, and you get a job at a local law firm as a new, young lawyer. You are most confident and know that you do a good job and that people like you. However, your drinking is getting a little out of control. You go into work, feel great, and get done knowing that you did a good job. This is the right mindset. You are sitting there thinking about how good you did today. Then, you leave, and your mindset totally changes. You get lazy and go home and uncork that wine bottle. You've now entered a much unhealthier mindset. What you need to do is learn to balance. There are mindsets that we can't detect and have a hard time fighting against.

Chapter 7: Positive Thinking, Confidence, and Motivation

Positive thinking is extremely important in holding your confidence and making peace with the world. Positive thinking is making the best of difficult situations, reframing difficult things, completing a grief process and holding yourself up through it. It is many things. Each of us will have a different relationship on what positive thinking is. There are deep and numerous reasons that you should learn to think positively. Our thoughts affect our bodies in a deeply intimate way. Both go back and forth; the body affects thoughts and emotions in a drastic way. When you learn to develop consistent negative thinking that brings yourself and others down, your entire being is affected in a negative way. Everything from your muscle tensions to your immune system will be weakened by the experience.

Ever heard the expression, "you are what you eat"? There is a variation on that phrase: "You are what you think." When you think negative thoughts about yourself, you are participating in a sort of self-loathing self-fulfilling prophecy. If you are always telling yourself that you are lazy and worthless, you encourage yourself to do types f behaviors that you consider worthless or lazy. You start to think about yourself as the worst version of yourself. This is something that needs to be battled against. Positive thinking is much better for your overall health. Positive thinking will improve your mood and attention span and even your physical health.

It all starts with a perspective change. You must think about yourself; "what do I criticize about myself? Why do I criticize myself?" You've got to first identify the ways in which you bring yourself down. This may be an easier process for some than others. Some people have body issues. They don't like the way they look, or they find that they are continually putting themselves and possibly others down for their looks in its extreme, this is known as body-dysmorphic disorder. This type of person will need to learn how to do two things: The first is to decide what they want to do, and are actually capable of doing, about their looks. This could be a practice of starting to jog or some other form of exercise. It could involve eating better. Whatever goes down, it just has to be something attainable and gentle. The second task is to let go of whatever you are holding that is negative about your appearance. You can just let that go and say, "I've been exercising lately, which is something that I can do to improve my appearance. That is enough work for me to do in this area." and forgive the rest. You've got to face that voice that is telling you look horrible and disgusting because that voice is essentially just you. Sometimes we have bullies or abusive people in your lives, and they tell us mean things about ourselves. Often, though it is coming from our own consciousness.

Positive thinking means that you are shifting from the perspective of bleakness and gloominess and starting to acknowledge the beautiful things that you do experience often times, it's not that there aren't beautiful experiences in our lives, but rather that we are not accessing the experiences that are right in front of us. Positive thinking means shifting just a little, from "It's dark out today and I don't want to go to work" to "its dark out today, but I am going to do my best at work and maybe take a nap afterward." It is not all sunshine and rainbows. Positive thing should be realistic and attainable.

Confidence will be greatly strengthened when you get into positive thinking. Confidence is something that is difficult to measure and difficult to grow. It comes from deep down in the spirit, and it knows that one can be kept safe and sound by his or her own will. Confidence comes from self-security. If there are a bunch of things that you hold in shame, like past experiences, or other sources of embarrassment, you will not find it easy to have confidence. To have confidence, you must let all that stuff go and admit to yourself that you are a person who is worthy of being listened to, hear, and understood, and then communicate yourself that way.

The best and most classic way to be confident is to be yourself and to own it. If you are a tall person, love that you are tall and share it with the world. If you are a short person, own it and love your shortness. There are all kinds of body traits and all kinds of people who love people with your body traits. Whatever mental or physical traits you might have insecurities about, you just have to give up on those anxieties and let go. It'll be better for you in the long run.

Motivation is extremely important to address for people with depression. Depression in large part very dependent on motivation. The lack of motivation is what drives depression, and often times this turns into a cycle of lack of motivation and negative feelings. Motivation is a nebulous concept, but we can pretty much say with confidence that when your body is healthier, you are generally more motivated. When you are spending all of your time on an addiction or in unhealthy habits, you are feeding this cycle, and your motivation will be cut short. This is unfortunate, but it happens.

A big part of positive thinking is learning to self-talk about good things and also to separate yourself from the bad thoughts. You can just let yourself know that thoughts are knot real. You don't have to disprove thoughts; you can just say that they are mean or unnecessary and do away with them. Lots of people out there pace way to much value on their thoughts, their tiny little thoughts, and their content, and they spend all of there time "strategically" thinking, as to bring out some kind of satisfaction. But the satisfaction never comes.

What is helpful for this situation is to learn how to tell yourself declarations. You are not your thoughts. Your thoughts only exist in your head. Sometimes they are correct, or true, and sometimes they are not. It doesn't matter. In either case, they do not make you up. You are not a good person or a bad person for what you think.

Thoughts just come through the mind; you don't generate them. Thoughts are a very abstract stream of consciousness that comes through in language or imagery. They are not real. You have the power to make them real; for example, if you have the thought of walking outside tomorrow in the sun, and then you take a walk outside tomorrow, you have thought of something and then made it real. However, it wasn't real until you did it. Thoughts are not accessible by other people, and they are your own personal psychic space. Now, you need to take care of that space, and be able to filter what you want to be a part of that space and what you want throughout. This is where you can train yourself to have a stream of new, positive thoughts. Start cultivating thoughts that bring you closer to your self-potential. Start rewarding yourself for being nice to yourself and others. Self-care is extremely important.

Positive thinking isn't something that you'll be able to pick up overnight. But if you practice being nice to yourself and being non-judgmental in your thoughts, you can start to make a shift in your thinking. You will find yourself with a more open heart, a wiser mind and a stronger soul.

Chapter 8: Anxiety and Procrastination

You must consider context when it comes to the treatment of mental health. We live in a certain time, a certain era where there are stigmas and norms in place. Unfortunately, there is a lot of stigma and shame around mental illness. Stigma is when people place moral judgments on other people for having mental health problems. This might take the form of scoffing or actual joking, or it may be subtler, like microaggressions or subtext in a comment. Mental health issues are sometimes seen as "weak" or "evil" or just embarrassing. This is a huge issue in mental health treatment at the moment. Stigma happens in different ways.

People lack the vocabulary to describe their experiences with mental illness. Someone with the onset of depression for the first time often will not be able to recognize their condition as a medical and mental health one, and may not end up receiving treatment for a long time because they simply didn't understand what was going on. This is caused, in part, by the lack of conversation around mental health issues. When people don't talk about their experiences with mental illnesses in their family, community, or school, it starts to be a subject that is avoided altogether, and this fosters a culture of silence around the issues that matter.

Stigma may be driven by shame for some people. People develop deep senses of worry and shame for their mental health symptoms; this may have come from internalized messages from family or society. People carry shame for a long time; some people never let it get into the light with their issues. They may be afraid that the world will abandon them if they admit they are not perfect, or they may just have a sense of being overwhelmed.

Shame and embarrassment may cause people to avoid identifying their treatment to the outside world. They may tell people that they have a doctor's appointment instead. Some people will share with close friends and family, o that they have decided to enter treatment, others will not. When you do share that you are receiving mental health treatment, you are normalizing the treatment and making it more accessible and seemingly safe for others to try. To defeat stigma, a difficult aspect that must be an achieved is for people in treatment to start talking about it.

One way to reduce shame and start talking about mental health treatment is to encourage equality between physical and mental illness. When people are diagnosed with diabetes or cancer, a certain respect is typical in regard to the disease. This is not always the case with alcoholism or schizophrenia. We have as humans a natural animal tendency to want to alienate the "weak"; it is a base drive of human nature and must be fought against with morality and reason.

Anxiety is a basic human trait; it has served an evolutionary purpose. Back before civilization was in full swing, our ancestors used to have to be extremely and delicately tuned into their environment. This meant that they had to be ready to defend themselves from predators or other people at a moment's notice. So our "cavemen" versions had a lot of anxiety, for good reason, because predators were chasing them down. This is all fine and good because it helped to protect them for danger, but we have enveloped since then to still have mostly the same anxiety responses, the stimuli are no longer there. There might be times when we need to defend ourselves from animals or other people, but most of sometimes, people's anxiety, which was meant to protect them, is not evolutionarily useful anymore in terms of their lifestyle and relatively high level of safety, and it just causes disturbances in life. This can cause people to be avoidant, to be isolated, and it can cause them to be nervous and shaky in all kinds of situations.

Anxiety is one of the great problems of millennials, which is now becoming adults. Anxiety stems from and causes worry. It is a physical state of tension that is often paired with negative thoughts or emotions. Anxiety is a state of being tense and too alert for the situation. Anxiety often comes from worrying about the future or the past, and it often can be paired with other disorders like depression or bipolar.

There are a few things that can help overcome anxiety.

One of them is mindfulness. That will be discussed later on. The other is relaxation. Relaxation is an important part of human life, and we often don't acknowledge its worth for our health. Sometimes relaxation is thought of as an overindulgent thing, but it is necessary and good for our health. There are automatic and manual impulses in our bodily function. For example, we can bat our eyelids willingly, when we want to wink at a person, but our eyelids will blink automatically when our sensory organs tell them that they are in danger, as well. So we have voluntary and involuntary responses, and you can use the voluntary ones to "trick" the body into relaxation. Breathing is a great way to use this theory to calm down the body and become more alert and focused and calm. By using deep breathing techniques, you can tap into the response that is provided by extra oxygen going to your brain. You can use that to manually calm down your body. Some studies show that deep breathing causes a relaxation response in the body. By forcing yourself to breathe slowly in and out, you are able to modify your body's function and slow down what is happening.

Try to make a list of things that you find relaxing. Finding things to relax you is a surefire way to defeat anxiety and get back on your feet.

Procrastination is a debilitating habit that gets to a lot of us; procrastination is that little voice that tells you its cool to do it later. It is a persistent voice, and procrastination has a lot to do with focus. When you aren't able to focus, your mind will get pulled easily from the task at hand. This brings you away from thinking about what you are doing and makes you start thinking about other things. Once you introduce the possibility of doing something else, you will experience a gradual tendency to start to do other things and say that what you started off doing is okay to leave for later.

So how can you start to combat this? Start demanding the focus that you want from yourself. This is a tough job and can lead to strain and struggle, but it will be worth it in the end. You can train yourself to focus; there are some things that you can also do to help yourself along the way. One of them is by eating, controlled amounts of food. Another is by taking breaks in between one task. You want to break down your task so that the whole task doesn't feel undoable.

Chapter 9: Mindfulness

The concept and practice of mindfulness is rooted in Buddhism. It is an integral part of the path to liberation presented by the Four Noble Truths and the Eightfold Path. Contemporary definitions of mindfulness usually include elements of receptive, present awareness and striving to forego being reactionary or judgmental.

There is some variance in ideas about the meaning of mindfulness. In some definitions, intentionality is emphasized. In others, there is a greater emphasis on wide and open awareness. Some definitions conceptualize mindfulness as an emotionally neutral process, while for others, like Thich Nhat Hanh, it can be closely linked with positive emotions like kindness or peacefulness. Henepola Guanarantana wrote that mindfulness is extremely difficult to define in words - not because it is complex, but because it is too simple and open. Thich Nhat Hanh, a Vietnamese monk, writer, and activist, describes himself when he is being mindful as being "completely myself, following my breath, conscious of my presence, and conscious of my thoughts and actions." A definition of mindfulness which can be useful for consideration in regard to its application in mental health comes from Jon Kabat-Zinn, the developer of Mindfulness-Based Stress Reduction, a program that integrates mindfulness into the treatment of a variety of health conditions. Mindfulness means paying attention in a particular way: on purpose, in the present moment, and nonjudgmentally. This kind of attention, Kabat-Zinn writes, can create greater skills of awareness, clarity, and a state of being present in whatever the present moment may be. Meditation can be understood as a formal practice of mindfulness, but mindfulness can be employed in seemingly all life moments and situations.

Mindfulness has influenced trends in psychotherapy in the past few decades in numerous ways. In the area of cognitive-behavioral therapies, there has been the development of MBCT (mindfulness-based cognitive therapy), which incorporates breath work and a perspective of awareness of body, as well as decentering from cognitions or feelings rather than trying to change them. Dialectical behavior therapy was originally fostered as a treatment for behavioral problems, especially people with Borderline Personality Disorder, and was created as a mindfulness-based therapy. It accentuates acceptance skills in the form of mindfulness and distress tolerance. The founder of DBT, Marcia Linehan, developed a schema of a 'divided' mind: the reasonable or analytic mind, the emotional mind, and the wise mind. In DBT, a goal for treatment may be to integrate an understanding of these facets. ACT, or Acceptance and Commitment Therapy, is another example of a contemporary therapy rooted in mindfulness.

You can start a basic mindfulness practice by focused breathing. Just sit in a relaxed place, and calmly let your body let go of its tension. As you sit, just notice how it feels to sit there and feel your body supported by the earth. As you become relaxed, start to shift your attention to your breathing. You can pay attention in any way that feels comfortable to you. You might place your attention at the openings of your nostrils, and just feel the cold on the inside of the nostril, and the heat of it as the air goes out. You might just put a hand on your stomach and feel it go up and down. Once you have some physical way to pay attention to the breath, see how long you can pay attention to it. At first, the time that you are able to focus maybe pretty short. This is okay; beginners are the best for mindfulness. It is all about coming back to your breath. Thoughts will come in; you can just let them leave and go back to the breath. You may feel distracting physical sensations; you may get distracted by sounds or thoughts. All of these will be gone in a few seconds, and you can just put your attention back on the breath.

Once you get a good handle on this, you can transition out of focusing on the breath and not an overall state of awareness. This brings the state of mindfulness to a full-body and sense level, where you are paying attention to each part of your experience, and being only present with yourself.

Mindfulness is a great tool for anyone trying to calm down their mind and get some sense of focus in their lives. Mindfulness can be a turning point for some people. Some people experience a range of whirling thoughts all the time and never learn to deal with it or talk about it until they learn about mindfulness. It gives people a third-person view of themselves, makes them detached and a little bit fairer to themselves and other people.

The thing is, we spend too much time attaching fully to our thoughts, and thinking can become an addiction in itself. Try this experiment: Imagine something, a scenario, or an event that occurred. Sit in a chair and close your eyes. Try to feel he temperature of the air in whatever place you are in. Try to see the sights and smell the smells. Try to hear what is happening in the place you are in. Try to feel the ground below you, know that the sky is above you, feel the wind or sound on your face if it is present. Now, snap back to reality. See our attention is a powerful thing. If you direct it at something, it will go there and stay there. We are able to direct our attention away from things as well. This is how thoughts and feelings become repressed: whenever we experience that thought or feeling, we direct our attention elsewhere and get distracted, and we are able to fix our situation in this way. By repressing, though, you do more damage. Where and when we place our attention is a really impactful thing. If you are always placing your attention on your thoughts, you will be a slave to your thoughts. Your thoughts are not physical. Your thoughts are not you. They don't control you; you control your thoughts. There might be times when your thoughts are very intrusive, and they might seem to control you, or even tell you that they control you, but they don't. They are just your thoughts.

Chapter 10: Helpful Links and References

National Alliance on Mental Illness:
http://www.nami.org

Psychology Today:
http://www.psychologytoday.com

UCLA Mindful Awareness Research Center
http://www.uclahealth.org/marc/

From An Ordinary Person: Mental Health Resources
https://mentalhealthresource.wixsite.com/faop

45 Simple Self-Care Practices for a Healthy Mind, Body, and Soul
https://tinybuddha.com/blog/45-simple-self-care-practices-for-a-healthy-mind-body-and-soul/

Introduction to Psychology 1
https://pressbooks.bccampus.ca/kpupsyc1100/chapter/history-of-psychology/

History Of Psychology (lecture)
https://www.youtube.com/watch?v=Dn7TrVIiQo8

Motivation (Lecture)
https://www.youtube.com/watch?v=791k5VVtmj0

TED Talk: The Puzzle of Motivation
https://www.ted.com/talks/dan_pink_on_motivation/up-next?language=en

Conclusion

"It's all in the mind."

— George Harrison

Why Psychology Is Important

In its primary form, psychology studies people—who and what they are. It looks into why they act and think the way they do and how someone can improve himself or herself. Therefore, everything a person does is connected to the subject.

Psychology allows people to understand more about how the body and mind work together. This knowledge can help with decision-making and avoiding stressful situations. It can help with time management, setting and achieving goals, and living effectively.

The science not only allows people to be more successful, but it can also impact their health. It helps many tackle their mental illnesses so that they can continue living their lives. Psychological studies have also aided in drug development and the ability to diagnose various diseases (such as Alzheimer's and Parkinson's).

"Through pride we are ever deceiving ourselves. But deep down below the surface of the average conscience a still, small voice says to us, something is out of tune."

-C.J.Jung

There are as many justifications to study psychology as there are students studying psychology. It's a personal choice. But here are five important reasons:

1. You Learn Why People Can Act Strangely

People are fascinating creatures! We all enjoy learning about the crazy things people do. This is what makes psychology, especially social psychology, fascinating. For instance, you will learn about the bystander effect, which explains why you are more likely to be helped when one person sees or hears you in your hour of need than when a large group is watching.

2. You Learn About Interesting Experiments

Many early scientific studies wouldn't pass the ethical test nowadays. Still, it's interesting to read about them.

One of the best known is the Stanford prisoners experiment, which studied the psychological effects of the power dynamic between prisoners and guards by having volunteers simulate a prison situation. Or that of Little Albert, a little boy who was taught to fear a little rat. Little Albert ended up being afraid of fluffy white animals for the rest of his life

3. You Learn to Do Research

Studying at university is cool because you learn academic skills. As a result, you end up with a more critical attitude, and you do not believe everything published or broadcast. And at one time or another, you'll get to do research about a topic of personal interest.

One of the most important tools that a psychologist has to his disposal is research. Research provides insight into human behavior, provided the psychologist makes use of scientific methods.

4. You Learn About Mental Disorders and Treatment Options

Many psychologists also deal with mental disorders and options for their treatment. Mental disorders are many and can have a debilitating effect on people's lives. Fortunately, various psychological treatments have been developed for many mental issues. Best practices have been written down in treatment and diagnosis protocols.

The prospect of being able to help others in their struggle to live a "normal" life appeals to many students.

The benefits of learning about mental disorders

5. You Gain Insight Into People's Behavior

Doing, thinking, feeling, and acting—as a student of psychology, you will get to study all aspects of human behavior. You will learn not only about the general characteristics of human behavior, but also about the differences.

What drives people? And how can you influence human behavior? These two questions are central to the practice. Examples of questions psychologists address include:

- How do people react to stress?

- Do athletes perform better after mental training?

- What is love, anyway?

- Why does one child perform better in school than the other?

- How is it that some of us are friendly and relaxed while others are often tense or stressed out?

In this book, we've looked at the contemporary understanding of basic psychology and its practical application. There are many concepts touched on in this book that you are encouraged to pursue in your personal studies. This doesn't have to be anything too intense, but if you choose one or two subjects that interested you from this book and research them a little yourself, you will be able to find out more in the areas that mean the most to you.